HE PRAYED

The Power of Prayer In Making Life Choices

How he did it, and how you can, too.

"Seek ye first the kingdom of God, and his righteousness; and all these things shall be added unto you."
Matthew 6:33

He Prayed

The Power of Prayer In Making Life Choices

How he did it and how you can, too.

George E. Winters

LAURUS BOOKS

Unless otherwise specified, all Scripture quotations are from the King James Version of the Holy Bible (KJV), which is available in the Public Domain.

Scripture taken from the NEW AMERICAN STANDARD BIBLE® (NASB), Copyright © 1960,1962,1963,1968,1971,1972,1973,1975,1977,1995 by The Lockman Foundation. Used by permission.

HE PRAYED
The Power of Prayer In Making Life Choices

BY GEORGE E. WINTERS

Copyright © 2013 by George E. Winters

All rights reserved. This book is protected under the copyright laws of the United States of America. This book may not be copied or reprinted for commercial gain or profit. The use of short quotations or occasional page copying for personal or group study is permitted and encouraged. Permission will be granted on request.

Paperback Book: ISBN: 978-1-938526-32-9
E-Book: ISBN: 978-1-938526-35-0

Published by LAURUS BOOKS
Printed in the United States of America

LAURUS BOOKS
P. O. Box 894
Locust Grove, GA 30248 USA
www.TheLaurusCompany.com

This book may be purchased from TheLaurusCompany.com, Amazon.com, and other retailers around the world.

Dedicated to all of the young people
who are learning to pray and listen
for the guidance of the Holy Spirit
in their life choices.

~ Matthew 6:33 ~

Chapter One

Circa 1954

William Ray Houston was twenty-six years old when he knelt by the side of his bed and prayed aloud. Since the time he had served in the Navy, most people referred to him as "William," or simply "Will." His family would probably call him "Billy Ray" forever. What he was called really did not bother him. It was more important that people thought of him as a man of integrity.

Tonight, William addressed his prayer to the Holy Spirit, firmly believing that Jesus Christ has ascended to the right hand of His Father and that He has sent a Comforter to be within those who accept Jesus as Lord and Savior.

The bed he knelt beside was in a single room with an attached bath, one of other such rooms in the building. It was small but homey and was a short bus ride to his job. He always paid his rent one month in advance. He couldn't afford an apartment.

William was a millinery buyer for a department store and had been transferred to St. Louis about a year before. Department stores didn't pay very much in those days, and they expected five and a half days' work, short lunches, and short vacations. They also had the policy of being open until nine on Thursday nights, as well as every night after Thanksgiving through Christmas. It wasn't a very attractive job, and the future didn't seem very bright.

William had befriended several of the traveling salesmen who called on him each and every season, so he knew a bit about their lifestyles. They made much more money, traveled their territory, had trips to major cities to pick up the line, plus expense accounts. It sounded much better than his humdrum nine-to-five department store life. And, they had a good time! He was still single, and their lifestyle appealed to him.

Kneeling beside his bed, he told the Holy Spirit what he wanted. He knew the Bible said that "the effectual, fervent prayers of a righteous man availeth much." Well, he didn't feel very righteous, but he was a very decent guy with good, if not high, morals. He was effectual, in that he was familiar with most of the Bible, thanks to a lifetime of Sunday school and church. In that period of time, pretty much everything had been covered. He was fervent, in that during the two and a half years in his uninteresting job, he saw no future. A strong, healthy, ambitious young man managing a millinery department? Ladies' hats? There was no excitement in that. Nor was it an appealing, interesting vocation to the young ladies he dated. It was certainly not exactly "macho"!

William prayed aloud each night, and the more he prayed the more articulate he became. He had two themes. The first was well defined. He yearned for a traveling job selling women's ready-to-wear. The second was for a wife. He was lonely living away from the home and friends he grew up with in Dallas.

Over time, as he prayed, it became clear to him that he was on the wrong road. It wasn't a bad road, but the direction was six hundred miles in the wrong direction, away from friends and family. Marrying a local girl there would pretty much seal that distance, and his parents were in their later years. He had an older brother and sister that he was close to, as well. If he was going to change jobs, it made sense to seek something in the area where his family was located. It was obvious that he needed to get off the department store road in St. Louis and go back to square one in Dallas.

He called his mother and made sure that it was okay to live with his parents while he sought work. He gave notice to the millinery company and drove home to Dallas with very little cash and very high hopes.

Chapter Two

Most of the ready-to-wear industry in Dallas took place in a variety of lofts and offices on or near Commerce Street, mostly on the southern end. William was pretty naïve. His former job had come from a college interview. He didn't have a résumé, so he just made personal calls from addresses in the Yellow Pages.

In the third week, he called on a well-known line of ladies' dresses and found a receptive ear. There was an aging salesman with a very good territory that could prolong his selling days with an aide. The aide would do the driving and carry the sample bags and, in the process, learn the ropes and get acquainted with the buyers. In time, the pro would retire, and the job would be his. But there were two problems with that. The first was that there was no telling how long that would be—years, perhaps. The second was that the sales manager had referred to him as their "token Gentile" in an all-Jewish company. This alone made him a little uncomfortable. Still, the experience would be invaluable. So again, he turned to the Lord in prayer. It seemed like this was the answer to his prayers, yet there was a lingering feeling he could not identify. After a lot of thought and prayer, William turned down the offer.

His search continued southward down Commerce Street

with little encouragement. Each morning as he drove into town, he felt a strange pull to drive to the Trinity Industrial District. This was odd because there were no ready-to-wear lofts in that area. By mid-day, however, he would find himself driving down the cross streets of the district. His money was running low, and he needed to do something soon.

One day, on an impulse, he stopped in front of a plastics distributor and filled out an application for a job. The interview went well, and with a handshake agreement to come back to talk salary, it was soon over. William felt pretty good as he opened the door to his car. Just as he sat down, he glanced across the street and noticed the offices of The Manhattan Shirt Company. He knew the company well. It was the distribution warehouse for the five-state southwest area. On the same impulse that got him to the plastics company, he walked across the street and introduced himself to a very attractive receptionist.

He didn't seek a job since he more or less already had one in his back pocket. Now, he was just a young man, formerly in department store retail, who was in the neighborhood and interested in the distribution side of the business. The receptionist introduced him to the manager, Fred, who gave him a few minutes of his time with a pleasant "get acquainted" visit, and that's all there was to it. He thanked the receptionist, handing her his calling card, and drove home. Late that afternoon, he received a call from the receptionist that the manager would like to see him the next day, perhaps around ten o'clock.

The manager's full name was Fred Gilson. He was a much older man who seemed very happy to see William. He invited him to sit down and began to explain their situation. The Manhattan Shirt Company had recently introduced a line of "man-tailored" shirts for ladies that were pretty new to the industry. The company had used their current sales force to introduce the line, but there were some problems with that.

For one thing, the salesmen only called on the men's department in the department stores they visited and on men's wear specialty shops. This meant that the ladies' blouses ended up in the men's wear area of department stores and in the wrong specialty stores. There was also the problem that there were only two seasons of men's clothing: spring and fall. Ladies' wear has always had four seasons, and Manhattan's salesmen weren't out there for the other two seasons. So even though the shirts were great, they weren't going over like they should. Having explained all this, Mr. Gilson got to the point, which was that they needed a ladies' wear salesman.

Mr. Gilson had an 8½ by 14-inch yellow sheet full of the names of men's wear salesmen that had applied for the job, but for all their experience they didn't fit the "ladies wear" image he was looking for. While William had never heard of "Lady Manhattan" or of man-tailored ladies' shirts, he talked department store ladies' wear language. In addition, the receptionist was very much taken with him.

In the end, William got a job with them, traveling a four-state territory selling this new style of shirts. It didn't take much for him to realize that this was exactly the job he had prayed for! He had a traveling sales job with a prestige line with no prior sales experience and not a bit of "road" experience, even though there had been dozens of more experienced salesmen up for the job.

It was a commission job with a base salary and a generous travel expense provision. Right away, Mr. Gilson cut him a check for $500 and gave him the name of a salesman at a better menswear store downtown. Gilson wanted William to dress right because he was representing a menswear company.

It turned out, too, that the receptionist had been praying for a husband. They married a year and a half later!

He prayed, and God gave him the very job and the wonderful wife he had prayed for.

Chapter Three

Within weeks, William found his new job to be all he had imagined from listening to those traveling salesmen. He had a four-state territory that took him to all the large towns and most of the smaller ones along the way. For the first year, he ate it up like chocolate candy. In addition to the sales calls, he took company advertising releases to the fashion editors of major newspapers in the respective areas. His personal visits paid off with free advertising in the fashion columns, which enhanced sales in the stores where he had sold the line. More and more, the company loved him, and twice a year when he went to New York for sales meetings, he was treated special. Life was good. He had been dating the attractive receptionist at the regional office, and there came a time when he looked forward to "home time" more than "road time."

William was twenty-eight when they married. His sales trips were often two weeks out, then back in for the weekend. When he was home, he wanted to be with his wife, which left little time to develop mutual friends. That was good for a year or so. He was alone most evenings, so he continued praying aloud at his bedside and sought direction for his life as a newly married man.

THE LIST

One Thursday evening after a hard week on the road, William pulled in to a hotel in Lake Charles, Louisiana. He was supposed to make calls in the city, work his way up the state, and return to Dallas by the following weekend. He slept well, and very early the next morning, with time to spare, he took some hotel stationery and made some simple notes. Then, for some reason he couldn't explain, he took a fresh sheet and wrote a heading—"WHAT'S IMPORTANT." He made a list and, still young in the marriage, placed his wife at the top of the list. Her name was followed by family, job, friends, God, neighbors, country (he had spent two years in the Navy, and that patriotism never left his heart), and a few other things that came to him as he wrote.

He didn't like the order of the names on the list, so he rewrote it and gave it some thought. For some reason, the list bothered him, so he knelt by the bed and offered his usual prayer. This time, once again, he included a request for direction. The morning was slipping away, and he wasn't dressed or ready for the day's sales calls, but he stayed there, ordered some lunch to be delivered—which was the only time in his life he ever did that—and even requested some more hotel stationery.

A list is an easy thing to make, and orders of importance are usually easily determined by expedience, convenience, time, and any number of other factors. But what is really, really important in life takes some deep thought. For example, you would think "wife" would be always be at the top. But if the country recalled him to the service in a draft of some sort, he would certainly leave "wife" and go serve "country." And "job" would seemingly always be near the top because that's how we pay for everything; it's how we survive. And for him, "friends" started near the bottom since he had very few because of his life on the road. But, as he made new lists, "friends" kept coming up again and again. He wondered why the idea seemed so important all of a sudden.

William did not leave the hotel at all that day, but the next morning his list was finished. God was at the top, "country" was next, "wife" was third, and "friends" came in fourth. His job, as good as it was, was farther down because he had realized how much this job got in the way of wife and friends. As he pondered all of this, he began making plans to change his life in the ways he was suddenly realizing were so important to him. He needed to get off the road. What had been so great and desired for so long was now losing its appeal.

You might wonder how a relatively short list could take the better part of a weekend for this young man.

What was really the main, persistent problem for William was getting and keeping God at the top of that list. It's an easy thing to pencil Him in, and some might think it's a "given." But when he thought of his life and his feelings, he was unsure and had trouble with it. At any given time, when all was well and things were going right, it was easy for him to think and feel a certain way about his life. On another day, however, he might think and behave a bit differently, seeing things another way. It seemed that his faith was tied up with his emotions, attitudes, and desires, but not truly at the forefront anymore.

But if God is truly at the top of the list, should his direction be elsewhere? Perhaps towards a ministry? William knew that kind of life was not his calling when he reviewed the other items on his list.

Then there were the other areas that just kept coming to the top of the list. What about them?

It took a lot of soul searching and serious introspection to get God firmly to the top of the list, but in the end, He was there. There was a Bible in the room, and with that Bible, our young man spent some considerable time reading and praying. Over and over, he found himself returning to the fourteenth chapter of John, and he tried to memorize the sixteenth and seventeenth verses.

John 14:16-17: *And I will pray the Father, and he shall give you another Comforter, that he may abide with you for ever; even the Spirit of truth; whom the world cannot receive, because it seeth him not, neither knoweth him: but ye know him; for he dwelleth with you, and shall be in you.*

> *It was The Comforter to whom he had prayed for all these years. He had prayed for a specific job and a specific wife. He had prayed for happiness and a life he could be proud of. And these things had been delivered. As he thought of this, when it was firmly fixed in his mind that the Holy Spirit of Jesus Christ was in him and with him, that was when he put God firmly at the top of the list.*

That list is with William to this day! It has made his life so simple. Whatever the issue, he could easily find the answer. If it was okay with God, do it. And if it was okay with God and with country, do it. And if it was okay with God, country, and wife, do it.

The point for William was that if it was not okay with God, that was the end of it right there. No further consideration was needed. And so on down the line. From the time he settled on that list, all of his decisions were easy to make.

Chapter Four

With his list of what's important firmly in his mind, William submitted his resignation from the company the Lord had led him to and began a new job search. He found a job that served as something of a "stop-gap" with the Dictaphone Corporation. It was not a good job, exactly, but it served its purpose. He was home every night, and the young husband and wife began developing a closer relationship, not to mention building friendships, which was an element lacking in their marriage.

Four years later, William was still at Dictaphone. He had been selling office machines, and the future looked like more of the same. He wouldn't have stayed so long, but he was very interested in the company. In addition, he was involved with The Dallas Junior Chamber of Commerce, which allowed him a degree of leadership.

TRIALS, TESTS, AND REWARDS

About a year into his job of selling for Dictaphone, William and his wife made two very big decisions. They bought a "starter" house in Garland, a close suburb of Dallas, and near the same time they decided to start a family. They began trying to have children, but months went by without any advances in that area. Not long after, his wife suffered from severe pain in her pelvis, so bad that she collapsed into painful sobs. They rushed her to the hospital and were told that things were very bad. She would need surgery, quickly, and it may require a hysterectomy. The night before the surgery, William again knelt by the side of the bed and prayed aloud. He asked the Holy Spirit of Jesus that the surgery would go well and that they would still be able to have children. He wanted a family. He wanted a baby boy. When he got up from the bed, he felt a calm he had not experienced before. You might call it serenity. He felt he had the assurance he needed. She would do well, and they would have a little boy one day.

At the hospital the next morning, with his mother and father by his side, William felt no apprehension at all. He was confident, but those around him were very tense, and it made him uncomfortable. So he took a walk outside and made his way down the street a block or so. It got his mind off the severity of the operation, and that was okay because he knew the outcome was all going to be good. He got back well before the surgery was over and waited with the family for the doctor's report.

A somber doctor came in to say that they had been forced to perform a complete hysterectomy, including the womb. She was going to be fine, but there would be no babies. William was greatly relieved about his wife but completely at sea about what he had thought was God's assurance of a son. That night, again at his bedside, he had a long talk with God. It wasn't so much a conversation, however, as it was listening. He asked, and he listened. Again and again. Once more, he experienced the same calm he had felt before, and he slept well. Their lives went on.

A few months later, during a follow-up visit to her physician, his wife mentioned adoption. The doctor smiled and said he thought he could help her with that. She came home excited, and he knew that whatever she wanted, he wanted, too. They had not even completed furnishing their home when the doctor called that he might have a baby for them. There was a young woman from a neighboring town who had two grown children from an ex-husband, and she was pregnant again. She was living temporarily in Dallas during the time her pregnancy "showed" and might be willing to put the baby up for adoption. The doctor made the arrangements for William and his wife to pick up her medical payments for the last third of her pregnancy and all hospital costs. Someone from an agency came to their home to interview them regarding fitness for adoption, and they passed with flying colors. It was all set. The baby he felt God had promised him was on its way, and he would be the father of a little boy.

A few months later, the doctor called to say that the delivery was excellent, the mother was fine, and they could go to the hospital to view their new baby girl. They were elated and excited on the way to the hospital. Yet, in the midst of their emotions, William was wondering what had happened to his answer from God. Wasn't he supposed to have a boy? But together they watched through the glass as their new baby gave them quite a show from her little white hospital crib. As if she were performing, she turned this way and that, raised her arms, and smiled with the fattest cheeks you ever saw. They were in love with her before she was in their arms. She couldn't have been more perfect.

They named her Lorrie, an abbreviation of his wife Sharon's middle name. Lorrie was the sweetest, most joyful and cheerful child you could imagine. Things went very well for the three of them for a long time. They were so determined to do things right, in fact, that they wore out a book by Dr. Spock about child rearing. In that book, there was a chapter on the "terrible twos," a passage that suggested it would be better to have a second child before the first reached three for several reasons. They mentioned this to the doctor who had helped with the adoption, and he said he would certainly keep it in mind.

William had been very active with the Junior Chamber of Commerce and chaired a committee that was putting on an event during the seventh inning stretch at the Dallas baseball game. The plan was to serve hot dogs and sodas to boys from a league the Jaycees had sponsored earlier in the season. During the "stretch," the boys were to come on the field and run the bases. It was a big night for them and the Jaycees.

William and Sharon had arranged for his mother to babysit Lorrie for that night. They were sitting in their den alone waiting when the phone rang. It was just before time to leave for the big event. As he got up to answer the phone, William knew this was no ordinary phone call. Before he picked it up, he felt it was something special. It was their doctor saying he had a little baby boy for them if they were interested. He was premature, which meant he was very small and still on oxygen, but he had been examined by a pediatrician and seemed to be in excellent health. William had called Sharon to him and explained what was going on, and together they said, "We'll take him." Overjoyed, they proceeded to the game with their hearts elated at the big news.

William had always received specific answers to specific prayers. He had a wonderful wife and two precious children. He felt that The Maker of the universe knew him personally, and he continued to always thank Him in his prayers. He often felt that the Holy Spirit of Jesus was within him and guiding him, and he tried to live his life accordingly.

Soon enough, William was thirty-five, with a wife and two children, and he had to think of the future once again. So, again, he found himself on his knees asking the Lord for direction, for meaning, and for purpose. He read the classified section every day, yet very little appealed to him.

A Jaycee friend who was doing very well as an insurance salesman had talked to him about something new that seemed attractive. His friend had specialized in car insurance and had insured most of the city's taxicab businesses. His company wanted him to put more emphasis on life insurance, but handling the taxi business was taking his full time. So, his insurance friend made him a deal that sounded great. The idea was that from the taxi and other car insurance business, his friend would furnish him the leads to make life insurance sales and help him along the way. It was a natural way to do it because they were already doing business with the company.

William was sorely tempted. Yet, he didn't seem to get the "go" feeling he had felt before. The chances were that he would have become a very wealthy man because his friend knew the business well and would have guided him with a personal interest. He also had a wide acquaintance base because of his involvement with the Jaycees. He had been Jaycee of The Year and a director twice. The last time, his portfolio won Portfolio of The Year among the larger Jaycee clubs.

In looking back at that period of time, he reflected that this may have been the path the Lord had laid out for him. It would have been a good life and in line with what he had prayed for when in St. Louis. He had prayed asking the Holy Spirit for the work he wanted to do and a good wife. With no prior sales experience and no travel experience, he had been given exactly the job he had prayed for, and he had soon thereafter been given exactly the wife he had prayed for.

Looking at himself that weekend, William reaffirmed his strong belief that God knew him. He would carry that realization with him all the days of his life. So, when he prayed about this opportunity with his Jaycee friend, he again looked for a specific answer. This time it didn't come.

In the end, he did not take the job. He wondered if not taking this route may have upset the Lord's plans for him or if it meant things may have had to be rearranged so that the Lord's Will in his life could come about in another way.

Chapter Five

ONE FOOT IN FRONT OF THE OTHER

At the time William had considered but turned down the insurance sales job with his friend, his brother-in-law, knowing that he was looking for work, suggested selling products that are often used up and replaced over and over. As an example he mentioned envelopes and stated that banks mail thousands of statements every month.

In the weekend classifieds, there was a help wanted ad for an envelope salesman. It wasn't something he had ever considered, but he approached it with quite a level of interest. On the very weekend that his in-law mentioned this specific field, there was a job opening for that very business. He applied on Monday and got the job almost immediately. He praised the Lord for yet another answered prayer and another new opportunity.

In the job application interview, he had stated that he was looking for something that would lead to sales management. He had a BA degree from SMU and hoped to put it to use down the line. The envelope company had several plants around the country. The nearest one was located in Houston, Texas. The sales manager in Houston was nearing retirement, which meant that a promotion might be in the cards. He thought the job was made to order, exactly as he had prayed for. He took it without hesitation and began work out of a small office in a building on Central Expressway. He called mostly on banks and insurance companies and opened many accounts in North and East Texas.

Shortly after two years in the Dallas market, the opportunity to go to Houston came up. With Sharon by his side, he was told that if he could develop a Southeast Texas market and sell in the Houston area, he would certainly be in line for the sales manager's job. Based on that conversation with the firm's president and Mail Well's general manager, they agreed to move to Houston.

It was not an easy decision. William's father was in a nursing home, though his brother and sister were able to visit regularly. His wife's parents were both elderly. She had frequent visits with them and her three sisters in the area. William was thirty-five, and the books he read always said you need to be on course with your business life by then. You have to be in the seat you want by forty-five because, at fifty-five, it's not likely you'll go further. Of course, there could be many exceptions to that, but he did have the initiative to think ahead. They agreed to move to Houston.

So the Lord had led him to a new job in a new city with a lovely wife and two children, and the future was before him.

In his second year with the envelope factory, before the move to Houston, the health of William's mother began to fail. Surgery revealed cancer of the colon, and she went downhill pretty fast. While she was in the hospital for the second time after the surgery, her heart began to race. William and his family were called to the hospital where the doctor stated that if they couldn't slow down her heart, she would die in intensive care. That was mid-morning. Stricken with fear, he went into the hospital chapel to be alone with his thoughts. It was a Catholic chapel with busts of Saints around the front and sides. There were kneeling rails, and he knelt there and again prayed to the Holy Spirit, begging Him to spare his mother. He sat in the pew and prayed again and reviewed Bible verses he had known since he was a child. Others came and went as the morning wore on, yet he stayed there. He may have dozed off in the quiet atmosphere only to awake and repeat his prayers again. He thought of a verse from the book of James, "The effectual fervent prayers of a righteous man availeth much," and he prayed yet again.

It was approaching noon, so he returned to the waiting room and joined his brother and sister. He sat in a chair across an aisle from his sister who was engaged in conversation with another woman. They were talking in such a way as to be mildly annoying when he suddenly sat up erect in his chair as a strange calm came over him. He instantly became confident that everything was going to be all right. Then the back of his head, from ear to ear, began to tingle, as if the flesh there had gone to sleep. It would have been disturbing, except it didn't last long. Within moments it was gone. He sat there and didn't think much about it.

Fifteen minutes later, the doctor came in. With a small smile, he told them that about fifteen minutes ago, his mother's heart had suddenly snapped back into a normal rhythm, and it seemed that she would be all right. William realized that his ears had tingled at the same time his mother's heart had returned to normal! In his mind, it was nothing less than a miracle. The family was greatly relieved, and several days later, she was allowed to return home.

While she was happy to be home, she was still very uncomfortable. Her health continued to decline steadily. He spent as much time as he could with her and read the Bible to her on several occasions. The family hired a caregiver, but as her health continued to decline, they knew she was unhappy. About two months later, she had to return to the hospital for the last time. She died there.

During the mourning period leading to and following the funeral, William had time to ponder on answered prayers. It seemed to him that the Lord God Himself had answered his prayer that his mother's heart might be set aright and that she might continue to live. It occurred to him that had he not intervened with his prayer, God would have let his mother exit this life in a quiet and comfortable way under the care of hospital specialists.

But God had answered his prayer, to his mother's detriment, and she suffered for two more months. It occurred to him that perhaps his prayer was more for his own benefit than for hers and that the Lord's Will in his mother's life would have resulted in a better end for her. This guilt weighed on him a bit, yet he felt a confidence that, to him, the Lord had, in fact, answered his prayer yet again. But, after witnessing his mother's suffering, he became much more careful about what he prayed for!

It was several years later, in a Sunday School class, that he read in 1 Samuel 3:11, "And the Lord said to Samuel, Behold, I will do a thing in Israel, at which both the ears of every one that heareth it shall tingle." Chills ran up William's back as he read it and knew that what he had felt in that waiting room was a direct message from God Himself. God did, in fact, know him personally and had given him a direct answer to his prayer. Again, he was struck by the resounding sensation that God knew him!

Over time, the job went well in Houston. He got along with the other salesmen, and he began to shine a little bit among them. It turned out the sales manager was not really a manager of sales at all. He was actually a sort of super salesman who had been there forever and had most of the best accounts. If the plant manager wanted to talk with the salesmen, he would have this ace man call a meeting; that was about it. The time he had spent with the Jaycees turned out to be an asset because he was accustomed to addressing a large group of people. He looked pretty good in those sales meetings.

In the past, a percentage increase in each man's sales was assigned and that was about it. He questioned management about what the company was going to do to help them attain those goals. Because he was so concise and determined, he got some concessions that the salesmen hadn't been able to get before. Then he offered a plan that motivated workers to exceed those goals. He gave them some numbers that showed them what their time was worth, which cut down their time at the coffee house down the street where they had a tendency to lounge. It was very common for most salesmen to work hard to meet their quotas but, having reached them, slow down and relax their efforts. He painted a picture of what they could do with commissions over and above their quotas. With this, he motivated them to work harder, and they all did well.

There was one office worker who received the salesmen's orders each afternoon and initiated their process through the plant. He was cheerful enough, but he tended to come around with a lot of "four letter words" and some extremely questionable jokes. Each time he would start up in this manner, William would get up and go to the plant to take care of his business there, leaving the joke unfinished and the worker aware that his humor wasn't appreciated. Slowly the message came across that the language wasn't appreciated, and, to make a long story short, the office environment became a much more comfortable place. It was a good job. It seemed to have a good future, and he was making enough money to buy a much nicer house in a modest neighborhood.

There was a Baptist Church nearby, and the whole family became involved in its Sunday school program. They were there Sunday mornings, Sunday evenings, and Wednesday nights. His wife helped in the nursery, and he became a substitute teacher for the adult classes. There were four men's classes in his age group, and each of the teachers worked with oil companies nearby that provided three-week-long vacations in the summer. So, while they were gone, he was pretty busy filling in during those summer months, though he never had a class of his own. The teaching experience required the use of Bible commentaries, which gave him a more meaningful insight to what the Bible has to say.

Again, he found himself making a list. He had kept his original list of what was important to him, but this one was different. That list had taken a great deal of thought and was revised a number of times until he got it right. Now he made another list, focusing on the important decisions he had made in his life.

My Life's Major Decisions

- Joined the navy
- College
- First job, which led to St. Louis
- Job change – back to Dallas
- Marriage
- Children
- Job change – Dictaphone

Actually, the list was pretty long. From time to time, he added another decision from the past. He kept that list nearby and referred to it sometimes when he was meditating. Looking back on those decisions and the events that led up to them, he could see God leading him along the way and could wonder about where he would be taken next. It gave him an incredible inner confidence. He was in the Lord's will and, like the other list, this one also kept him on the straight and narrow.

So, with his priorities straight once again and the money sufficient, life was good, and the years flew by.

A few years into the job with the envelope factory, the "super-salesman" was getting older, and it was evident that a bona fide sales manager was needed. William had little doubt that he was in line for the job. Unfortunately, his back had been giving him a lot of trouble; the pain was running down into his hips, and he was often very uncomfortable. It's hard to be cheerful and upbeat when you're in pain, and it began to show. He wasn't at his best for several months, which eventually led to back surgery and a month or so of recuperation. In the sixties, invasive surgery was pretty tough. He had three ruptured discs. The wound was long and deep, and took quite a while to heal. It was probably six months or so from "bad back" time through the long recovery after surgery. During that time, the company decided to hire a sales manager from a rival company. In the end, the sales manager's job he had moved to Houston for was gone, and at thirty-eight, the prospects of sales management looked mighty dim. It seemed it was once again time to set a new goal in life.

Chapter Six

A STEP OF FAITH, A BUSINESS OF HIS OWN

William had a friend at church who was looking to buy a major franchise and was attending the business and franchise shows that periodically passed through major cities like Houston. Curious, he went with his friend to several of these shows, which, in time, led him to think about owning his own business. If management was what he really wanted, his own business would certainly provide that. The trouble was that the franchises his friend was looking into involved many, many thousands of dollars and were way out of his reach.

About the time that he had been having back surgery, his father passed away. Afterward, his part of the estate was a little more than eleven thousand dollars. Doesn't sound like much today, but at that time, three thousand would buy a brand new Pontiac. Among the franchises that were presenting, there was a rinky-dink vacuum forming sign machine. It had a Hoover motor to create a vacuum under a thin sheet of styrene plastic. By spelling out some copy with plastic letters and forming the plastic over it, a three dimensional sign was created. Roller-coating some paint over the surface of the raised letters left you with a very different sign from what was usually offered with a paint brush. Best of all, it required little to no skill at all but created a unique product. William decided to give it a try.

He went to several sign shops, where he got the address of the leading sign magazine and subscribed. In the library, he found material that described the vacuum forming technique in detail. With subsequent visits to the sign shops, now talking the language a little, he found there was no company making larger, backlighted sign faces in southern Texas. While he was looking into this, a group of guys bought one of the franchises in Pasadena. The only thing they really bought was one of the rinky-dink machines because there were other much better machines on the market, and they had no area protection. So he struck a deal with them to fill his orders, got some samples, and went out to try selling signs. He was pleased when he found that he was indeed able to sell them. He was still working at the envelope company during this time, so all of this was done on the side.

Not long after, there was an ad in the trade magazine he read for a much larger vacuum forming machine that could be financed by the company. He made the deal, flew to their site for two days of instruction, and at their suggestion, went on to Eastman Chemical for another day of instruction. There he learned about making the molds upon which to form the plastic. When he got home, he had to select a site, buy materials, and buy tools, most of which he had never used before. Here he was, setting up a sign business from scratch with virtually no sign experience and no experience actually running a business, not to mention that he had precious little cash. Surely disaster lay ahead.

Most evenings, all day on Saturdays, and after lunch on Sundays, he was at the shop getting the business started.

During one week of his set up, there was a three-day sales

meeting in Dallas. While he was there, he finally realized that he would have to resign from his job at the company. Things were not going well at the shop. The money was running low, and it was time to give it his full attention. A lot of his money had gone out in this venture, and very little was coming in. He went back to his knees in prayer, addressed the Holy Spirit, and sought direction.

He resigned from his job at the envelope company.

While he had been with the envelope company, he had called on a man who handled the mailings for a service club. The man invited him to visit the club, and he subsequently joined the club and attended the weekly luncheons. One day while in his shop, the man walked in for a surprise visit. He had just come from a meeting at the club's main project. William asked his friend what brought him to the area and was told that on the way home, he felt a sudden compulsion to come see how the sign shop was doing.

This friend got quite an earful! A wife, two children, a mortgage, a lease payment on the machine, rent on the sign shop, and not nearly enough time to bring in the sales. It was a little bit depressing, but his friend had an interesting reply. He had just sold his business and had not yet invested all of the proceeds. With a smile, he offered to move the cash the sign company needed from his account to the company's account. Not a loan and not a gift, just a transfer of funds from one place to another, no interest. He just asked that it be transferred back when the business was on its feet.

Was this the direction William had prayed for just a while before? He didn't take the offer at that moment, but he slept better that night knowing he had help for the asking. Jesus Christ had to have put it into this man's heart to come by that day and to make such an offer.

He knew then that help was on its way!

So, still on his knees praying for direction not long after, an opportunity came from Exxon. They were unhappy with the vendor who supplied the small plastic signs over the entrance doors to their local service stations. The signs used the same plastic letters that he was using for molds for his signs. From large sheets of Plexiglas, he could cut the background to size, spell out the copy, and solvent weld the letters to the plate. Then he would package the signs and send one to each station by UPS. It was doable, marginally profitable, and provided cash flow, not to mention that it was an entryway to Exxon and their business. The one problem was that it took time away from other aspects of the business and other more profitable efforts.

So here he was praying to the Holy Spirit, again, thankful for this small niche help and asking for a solution to the time it took away from developing the business. One morning, not long after, a man shuffled in looking for work. His arms and fingers and knuckles had knots on them from severe arthritis. He explained that he could work part time for minimum wage, or anything really. He just needed something to do and could use some cash. Once again, he was a specific answer to prayer.

They got a special table with racks to hold plastic letters, a stack of sign blanks, and they would solvent weld the letters to the blanks. Together, they could fill and ship thirty signs a day. William was again able to spend his full time on the sign business. That sign order with Exxon lasted for several years. When it was eventually cancelled, the old gentleman with the severe arthritis passed away a few months later. Though he was saddened by his loss, it felt as if the Holy Spirit had provided a solution for each man's needs when they needed it.

As the requests for the nameplate signs were winding

down, he prayed for a replacement for that business. Exxon was pleased with his service, and they had a need for a small backlighted sign to go over the service areas that simply said "Service." The need was put out for bids, and his small shop with little overhead managed to get the contract. There was a guy at the sign supply that knew all about wiring fluorescent signs and gave him wonderful explanations of what and how to build the sign Exxon needed. It was not a big contract but the individual orders came in at about the same rate that he was still able to make them. He shipped those to stations all over the country.

William could not afford experienced full-time help, so he hired a high school student to come in after school. While coping with Exxon's signs he was developing a reputation for making magnetic car door signs on the side. They were easy to make, and he and his helper could turn them out about as fast as he could bring the orders in. He finally began to get a few dollars ahead.

William's wife, Sharon, stayed at home with the two children but would often come in while they were in school to do the books and give him time to run errands. While the children were in grade school, her time at the shop was limited to a few hours. When they went to Junior High, she could stay until mid-afternoon. The business began to do much better with her presence there, but time was quite a problem for them. A realtor only has to sell houses, not build them, and an insurance salesman only sells policies. William had to sell the sign, get his supplies, make the sign, often deliver the sign, and then collect for the work.

Ever in prayer regarding his needs, it became clear to him that his main contribution was selling, but selling took his precious time. Often, he would have a poor month of incoming business, so he would go out and bring in some business. But then, while turning out those signs he had sold, the sales would fall off again, leaving him with a good month of sales followed by a poor month.

Eventually, he began making lists again. He used an 8½ by 14-inch yellow notepad and listed the things he had to do. Each morning he would list them and rank them by order of importance. If he was taking care of the top four, then he was making good use of his time. He also did his best to multi-task. If while he was in the area of dealing with #1 he could swing by and take care of #7 and #9, it made him that much more efficient.

In those days, he paid his young assistant six dollars an hour, and it was important that he was spending his own time engaged in far more than six-dollar work. Much of the time, that yellow pad had thirty or more things for him to do each day. With proper use of that notepad and his wife at his side, he began to make a little progress. After a few years of just making ends meet, he finally had several months of Exxon business that put a surplus in the bank.

He used that money to make a down payment on an owner-financed home that backed up to a major freeway. He cleared the backyard and put in a portable office building that attached to the back door of the house. He built a concrete parking area that merged with the access road to the freeway and had himself a high-traffic retail location. Now business could come to him. He revamped the business to also sell flags, pennants, and banners, and he hired full time help.

For the first time in quite a while, he had the time to consider the future and formulate some long-term plans. He tried several.

First, he hired a few part-time salesmen. He soon learned

it took more time managing them than they were worth.

After that, he put sign displays in office supply stores and gave a discount to the stores to promote them. This also proved not to be worth the effort.

He tried joining the Advertising Specialty Association, and some of their products fit well with his signs and services. With his traffic location, he put ad specialty samples in showcases and took orders when customers came in for signs. He sold T-shirts, baseball caps, calendars, and other things of the sort, and he didn't have to make them! This worked out very well, and, with ad specialties, the business grew.

When he had a little extra money, he bought a residence on another major freeway, converted the house to a showroom, and hired a full-time employee to run it. The idea was to sell signs from there and make them at the first location. The plan was good, but he could not find honest help and soon closed it down. He had originally bought the property on an owner-financed loan over ten years. It had a huge billboard in the back yard that provided an income from its yearly lease. After the second year, that lease expired, and he was able to renew it for substantially more money. When he closed the store, he rented the property to a guy who started a used furniture business with it. The rent from this tenant, plus the lease on the billboard was a good deal more than his monthly payment, and it all seemed to work out.

Later, he purchased a small house across the street from his first freeway store. Because of the flailing economy, he managed to get it for half the original price and rented it out for a small profit that suited him once again.

At one point, he arranged to import a jellybean dispenser through the Advertising Specialty Association. President Reagan was fond of jellybeans, so they made the news from time to time. He put out a four-color photo ad for marketing the dispensers in a national multi-card mailing. In the end, however, the returns didn't pay for the cost of the ad. He was glad he tried it, but never again.

The above, along with many more twists and turns, occurred over a total of twenty-seven years in the sign business he had started with no experience and precious little cash. William and his wife had put both children through college and sent them out into the world. With Sharon's help, they had bought and paid for three rental properties and paid off the mortgage on their own modest home. His wife had taken some travel vacations to Europe with her church groups, though he had always stayed home to tend the store. In the end, he did not take a single vacation in his entire twenty-seven years in business.

Chapter Seven

A Door Is Opened

William had stayed active in his Baptist church and, over a period of time, had several responsibilities. He joined a group of sixty within the church who met on Thursday nights, as well as a few weekends, for a church retreat. The topic, with a book and tapes on the subject, was "How To Be A People Helper." He never missed a meeting, although sometimes he had to sit far back because he had to come right from work. He absorbed the lesson material with great interest.

With a church membership of twenty-two thousand, there came a time when the church had a problem with their hospital visiting. The staff ministers were few, and there were many, many hospitals spread out over a huge area of greater Houston. Visiting all those hospitals took time away from the ministers' other church duties. Since Houston was a center for specialized treatments, numerous requests from churches in other states came in when one of their members was in a Houston hospital. So the church arranged for deacons to make those visits in teams of two. Each team was assigned an area within greater Houston and its suburbs. The church, during every Wednesday night service, would distribute a "hospital list" showing members in nearby hospitals, and those from other areas that they knew of. The teams would use that list to make their visits, greatly alleviating the staff ministers' workload. It turned out that his sign shop was near a hospital district, so he would visit alone and pretty much gave Thursdays over to making hospital visits. There were a number of times when the situation called for a woman's touch. At those times, William would call his wife who would quickly drop what she was doing and come right over to help. When he retired he gave much of his time to church activities.

Retirement

When William reached age sixty-five, he finally put the business up for sale. He was more interested in what he was doing in lay ministry, and time was passing his business by. Newer, more sophisticated equipment was on the market, and it cost a lot. At his age, he didn't want to invest what it would take to stay competitive, and retirement appealed to him. It took two years to find a buyer, but at the age of sixty-seven, he was officially retired. He spent his time playing golf and spending time with his church.

Some of those Thursday afternoon hospital visits required callbacks, so he tended to be at one hospital or another pretty often. That's the way he spent the next few years, with good friends from church, golf, and hospital visits.

He became very confident with his visits. He had some remarkable experiences that convinced him this was his calling. The whole situation often gave him the feeling that he was in the Lord's Will. There were seven major hospitals in the area, all within walking distance from one another if you followed the oval. And people had come from far off places to visit them. M.D. Anderson was world renowned as a cancer treatment center. Texas Crippled Children's was world famous, too. People would come from all over to Saint Luke's Hospital for heart related problems.

William would start at M.D. Anderson around ten in the morning, which gave the nurses time to deal with the morning's agenda. On most days, he had completed his visits by 3:30. He wore a badge that was the same as the clergy used, and he was registered with the complex, which enabled him to go almost anywhere clergy could normally go. His badge said "Deacon Ministry," but no one seemed to notice the difference. He was much loved in the hospitals and seemed to have a feel for patient's needs. Most visits were brief, but most of the patients were so relieved to have someone there who cared that it was good enough. He seemed to have a sense of timing: when to be there, when to follow up, what to say, and how to say it. He felt he was under the direct supervision of the Holy Spirit of Jesus Christ. His prayers in the hospital rooms seemed to be just what was needed, calling for courage, for healing, for peace, and sometimes a renewed relationship with Jesus. The patients he visited were comforted, and he left the rooms with joy in his heart and, sometimes, a lump in his throat.

It was a great time in his life. Both of their children had graduated from college and had very good jobs in Dallas. He was well liked in church and finally had many friends to dine with. He played golf regularly with his close friend, Henry, and their group. On Tuesday mornings, he attended a senior prayer meeting at nine o'clock and then swam laps at a nearby club. That was usually followed by a fast food chicken sandwich and an afternoon visiting the homebound members of his church. Thursdays were for hospital visits, and life was good.

Chapter Eight

THE MOVE

While brushing his teeth one Saturday morning, William looked in the mirror, and a thought came from nowhere. It was as though it was a very special message. The thought was that both of their children were in Dallas and all of their relatives were in or near the Dallas area, but he had drifted away from his lifelong home. He was seventy now, and it was time to draw nearer to family while he and his wife were both young enough to make a major move. He had seen hundreds of elderly folks lying in nursing home hospital beds alone and lonely with no family checking on them.

He had also seen how old age could confine an otherwise active person from their former friends. He was getting older, and the distance was beginning to bother him. He mulled it over for about a week and decided he would approach his wife with the thought of moving to Dallas. They were so happy in Houston that he thought it might take a while for her to come around to it.

On an early morning walk around the block, William brought up the subject. Sharon didn't hesitate. It turned out that the Lord had been speaking to her as well. As much as she loved her lifestyle in Houston, she wanted to be with her children and family. She had been so close to their children and visited them often, but it wasn't enough. They had two children in Dallas; he had a brother, and she had three sisters and a host of nieces and nephews. They prayed together, each in their own way, and spent almost every other weekend in the Dallas area looking for a new place to live.

They placed their rental properties for sale first, and within a few months, they were sold. As proprietors of a very small business, they had not been able to put very much aside for retirement. They had put both children through college and given each a new car as they started their first real jobs. But the sale of these properties and their home gave them quite a sum to put toward their new future. They bought a house in the greater North Texas area, paid cash, and invested the rest in the stock market. All of this took the better part of six months, and each day was bathed in prayer for God's will and direction. The house they chose was perfect for them, the neighborhood was great and they found a wonderful church to attend. They were seventy years old now, and ready for this new life and new friends.

As soon as William joined the church, he joined their homebound care ministry and began making visits to two of the area's nursing homes. It was just like old times. Their son came to visit almost every weekend, and their daughter came whenever she was in town. Sharon spent one day each week with her sisters and time with their daughter when she wasn't working. After a while, she began making visits with him to the nursing homes, and with some other volunteer work, they kept as busy as they wanted.

When William's brother passed away later on, he was glad that he had so much extra time with him because of the move. The years were all family oriented and went by quickly. His son loved to travel, and he planned vacations for the four of them. They went to Alaska and to the Fiords of Norway. They took motor trips to California, Seattle, and New England. Once, they took a trip with their son to meet their daughter in Atlanta while she was there on business. From there, they took in the eastern seaboard. They had wonderful, memorable times together.

In church, after quite some time, William became a substitute teacher for a small Sunday school class. This led to his becoming a leader of the Sunday school department. The main duties of a department leader were to set the mood for the class members and to let them know what was going on in the church. Each week, he arranged for various staff members to visit and give a ten-minute description of what they were doing in their area. He brought in some outside programs, such as the head of the downtown Senior Citizens Center, as well as leaders of several local volunteer services. To improve members' moods, he made an effort to visit in their homes on Saturdays to get to know them on a more personal level. That went slowly, since many weekends were spent with his family. Now in his mid-seventies, he was a pretty busy guy. And he loved it.

Chapter Nine

THE CLOUD

In the mornings, when William was outside getting the paper, he would look to the sunrise and whisper a prayer. Mostly, he would thank Jesus for another day, for His presence in their lives, for his wife and children, and for those he had lifted up in prayer the night before. It was a good way to start the day.

There was one late summer morning, however, when he went for the paper and the cheerfulness wasn't there. It seemed as if everything was going great. It was a beautiful day, and, as the Robert Browning poem, *Pippa's Song*, says, "God's in His heaven—All's right with the world!" But something was not quite right. It was not a feeling that stayed with him always, but it was there from time to time as days went by. And it became more frequent as time passed. Everything was great, yet he was concerned about something. This feeling stayed in the back of his mind, and he couldn't put his finger on it. When he went for his yearly check-up in the fall, he mentioned it to the doctor, but try as he might, he just couldn't describe the peculiar feeling. The doctor gave him a referral to a psychiatrist, but he didn't go. Perhaps the feeling was akin to depression, but he had nothing to be depressed about. On into the spring, he was like a cartoon character with a little cloud over his head. Something was not quite right, but he didn't know what it was. He had mentioned it to his wife, and she was aware of his concern, but she had no idea how to help, other than to pray for him nightly. During the following summer, it became more intense. The little cloud became a dark thunderhead. He decided to adjust his lifestyle in an attempt to change it.

First, he resigned his leadership role in the Sunday School program. It could be that his efforts were not appreciated here as they had been in Houston. His personality was more effective in a one-on-one basis than as spokesman to a group.

After that, he and his wife had a lawyer prepare a formal will and a "living will." There was no particular reason, but it could be that since the family often flew out for vacation destinations, a plane crash was possible, and he had an urge to be prepared.

Then he sold about half of their stock and bought staggered CDs that were FDIC insured. Perhaps there could be a market crash. At this stage of life, he should concentrate on preservation of capital rather than accumulation of it.

Each of these steps made him feel a little better about the future, but the ominous feeling persisted. Summer came and went, and when he had his yearly check-up, the doctor didn't mention it and neither did he.

On October 14, 2006, on her forty-seventh birthday, they had a special birthday dinner for their daughter, Lorrie. She was so precious to them. From the time she was three years old, Lorrie would decorate the Christmas tree. As time went on, she did a marvelous job of that and all things ornate. Her hobby was stained glass, and she had made countless beautiful, ornate window decorations for them, not to mention the lamps and knick-knacks she had made that were all over their house. She and her mother loved to shop together, and that alone had been worth the move from Houston. Most of their clothing and every household item had been purchased at one time or another on those shopping trips. She was so attentive to them that she brought a memento trinket from every major business trip she took. Lorrie had risen in the ranks in her corporate life and was the manager of a small department that dealt with lots of money. She was paid very well and was buying her own house and had even paid off her car. She had several groups of friends who liked to travel, so she was always doing something interesting, and her parents loved to have her come to visit. They were very proud of her.

On October 29, William and Sharon were dressing for Sunday services when the doorbell rang. It was much too early for visitors, so together they approached the door with a bit of trepidation. Their son stood on the doorstep with bloodshot eyes and tears on his cheeks. He collapsed into his mothers arms and whispered, "She's in heaven, Momma. She died last night."

It took a few seconds for what he had said to sink in, and then she began to cry. It was a terrified, wounded sob, and William had never heard anyone cry like that before. He and his son walked her to a living room chair and sat her down before they both knelt down beside her and cried as well. His mind went blank, and most of what he could feel was deep concern for his wife. Even in the movies they don't cry like that. It was a long time before they were able to compose themselves enough to ask about what happened. With his wife still sobbing, his son explained that he had been awakened in the night and called to come identify his sister's body. They said his sister had been with a group of friends at one of their homes. She excused herself to the bathroom, and when she didn't come out, they knocked on the door and got no response. It must have been a formidable bathroom door because someone had to climb through the outside bathroom window and found her there, dead. Among the guests was a couple who were both police officers, but, apparently, it was too late for artificial respiration. They were the ones who called for the police and an ambulance, though they knew it was too late.

As they knelt in the living room with his wife wailing and tears running down his face, it occurred to William that this is what that ominous feeling had been about. Some intuition had forewarned him that something was going to happen; something was going to interrupt his quiet, idyllic life. They talk about five senses, but now he was aware that there might be more than that. He wasn't able to describe it to the doctor or his wife, and his prayers never revealed it. Yet, he had known something was coming, and he took the only steps he could think of.

It was out of his control all along, yet there was a Presence that wanted him to know it was coming. It was the same Presence that, long ago, had him step across the street to the job and wife he had prayed for. It was the same Presence that he had prayed to and that had led him along for all of his seventy-plus years. It was that Presence that gave him the holy urge to visit hospital patients and care for those in need. A loving God was preparing him for an unpleasantness that was on the way. He made a mental note to know even more about Jesus Christ.

Their son, now in his forties, took care of all the funeral arrangements and looked after his parents graciously. There were far more people at the funeral than he would have imagined, but his son knew how many lives Lorrie had touched and had arranged for an adequately-sized sanctuary.

Somehow, they got through it. William had every confidence as to where she was now, and he had to hold on to that fact. He and his wife had given her a college education, a car when she graduated, and so much more, but she had no use for those things now. From infancy they took her to Sunday school and church on Sunday mornings and evenings, and even Wednesday nights. She was baptized when she was twelve. They gave her a Christian education and introduced her to Jesus Christ. He was comforted in knowing that she would be using that through eternity. As much as they missed her, they knew she was in a better place!

Following through on his resolve to know more about Jesus, he read several books on death, heaven, out-of-body experiences, resurrection, and the like. It didn't take him long to revert back to the King James Study Bible he had been using since he was twenty-seven years old. His mother had given it to him, and, over the years, he had filled the front and back blank pages with small, hand-printed notes from Bible studies and sermons. He started with Matthew and read through Revelation, then started again with Luke and went through Revelation. Then he started again with Isaiah and went through the Bible again and did the same starting with Jeremiah.

All of this took place over a period of several years but with a persistent hope to know His Savior better. His church started an eight-week study on Tuesday nights that dealt with the subject of heaven, based on a book someone had recently written. He didn't agree with some of what was said; many Bible verses were ignored. Much was assumed from our bodily perspective that may not be so in heaven at all. He knew that what the Bible describes is only what our very limited senses can perceive. For example, Heaven's streets lined with gold, and beauty described as rare beautiful gems. It all may be far more beautiful than that! In our minds, that's as beautiful as it can get, but heavenly beauty may be much, much more. With Lorrie's recent passing, he was acutely attentive to the book that was used in the course and to the comments that were made. He had a complete set of New Testament commentaries, and he read them through, this time centering on the subject of resurrection. He read it with a pen in hand, taking notes and following the references noted in the margins when verses referred to the subject of the resurrection.

William did not claim to be a scholar. He didn't go to seminary, nor did he have the credentials to speak, but he did his homework and stayed the course. He had been convinced that Jesus Christ knows each and every one of us. He had felt the Lord's presence all through his life and was comfortable telling anyone that Jesus is the Way, the Truth, and the Life.

William is in his eighties now and living quite comfortably with his wife of fifty-plus years. They live in a nice home in a nice neighborhood. They have traveled with their son to places near and far. Most of their activities are church related, and they each have pretty busy lives.

He was just an average guy who lived an average life. His little company didn't grow into a franchised chain worth millions. The only really notable thing in his life is that he knows the Lord, and the Lord knows him! And that is the greatest blessing of all!

PART TWO

PART TWO

How To Do It

There are seminars featuring renowned speakers who charge twenty dollars or more to hear how to do just what William did. There are dozens of books, each with hundreds of pages, eloquently describing how to succeed in almost any specific endeavor you can imagine. They are usually detailed and very thorough.

William's plan is deliberately simple and should work for anyone, whether starting a business or starting a marriage. He was a very ordinary man with no great accomplishment. He lived a good life and stayed close to Jesus Christ.

The following is a very plain explanation of how he did it and how you can, too.

1. **The first step is to be on the right road!**
   The right road is to know Jesus Christ as your personal Lord and Savior.

   He assessed who he was and proceeded confidently.

   Matthew 6:32-33: *"... for your heavenly Father knoweth that ye have need of all these things. But seek ye first the kingdom of God, and his righteousness; and all these things shall be added unto you."*

Answered prayer! The job, the girl!

2. **He put his life in God's hands and let Him lead the way.**
   He made his decisions and started down his new road.

   You have to start!

   Matthew 7:7-8: *"Ask, and it shall be given you; seek, and ye shall find; knock, and it shall be opened unto you: For every one that asketh receiveth; and he that seeketh findeth; and to him that knocketh it shall be opened."*

3. **He made lists.**
   It was clearer to him in black and white! Put it on paper so you can set it firmly in your mind. You want to get the main thing settled so you can concentrate on the next most important thing. Most hash it over and over, changing their minds every time they think about it.

   Don't let it confuse you; settle it!

   Habakkuk 2:2: *"... Write the vision, and make it plain upon tablets, that he may run that readeth it."*

TWENTY-YEAR PLAN

Envision what it is to be...

	ADVANTAGES	DISADVANTAGES
1. Twenty+ years from now	XXXXX	X
2. A ten-year goal	XXXX	X
3. A five-year goal	XXX	XX
4. A one-year goal	XX	XX
5. How and where to start	X	XX
6. Start!	XXX	X

Proverbs 19:20: *"Hear counsel, and receive instruction, that thou mayest be wise in thy latter end."*

Obtain all the information you can about what you want to do before you start. Be very sure you want to do this. Be very sure you are able to do it.

When you consider a change in your life, you need to envision what you want it to be at the end of the road. This is why you should have a twenty-year plan as well as one-, five-, and ten-year plans on how to get where you want to be. Sometimes, along the way, things don't work out. But with a long-term goal, you can make adjustments and still get there.

James 1:5: *"If any of you lack wisdom, let him ask of God, that giveth to all men liberally, and upbraideth not; and it shall be given him."*

4. **He kept daily contact, through prayer, with his Lord who had control of his life.**

God has led you to a plan for your life. If you're confident it's His plan for you, stick to the plan! Assess your situation. You may be right where God wants you to be. Count your blessings, name them one by one. If you are comfortable and happy and your future is secured, you may be right where God wants you!

There are temptations along the way. Particularly early in life, there are options. Each, in its own way, will affect your life—sometimes for just a few days, sometimes for the rest of your life. To stay on track, you must have a long-term plan, and your daily decisions should be based on that plan.

Keep your life linked up with the Lord.

Jeremiah 29:11: *"For I know the thoughts that I think toward you, saith the LORD, thoughts of peace, and not of evil, to give you an expected end."*

5. **He kept busy.**

   A family life. A social life. Service to man, and service to God. Each should be in its own proportion. You want the right balance. It's the way to grow into the man or woman that God wants you to be.

   There are those who have the urge to do something different with their lives because of too much idle time. Use the life you have in the best possible way. Properly used, it could be great where you are right now!

   Idle hands are the devil's workshop.

   Romans 12:2: *"And be not conformed to this world: but be ye transformed by the renewing of your mind, that ye may prove what is that good, and acceptable, and perfect, will of God."*

6. **He made decisions.**

   When one door closes, it's very likely that, in time, another door will open.

   He identified values that correctly aligned with long term goals. He assessed where he was, and he determined to get where he wanted to be. He knew what he wanted and asked specifically for it through prayer.

   Get the facts! Read up on what you want to do. Pay a visit to those who are now doing whatever it is that you want to do, and ask lots of questions. You want to be sure that what you are contemplating is what you really want to do. Some roads look good until you've been down them a little ways.

Then, after you've done this, when you really believe it, act on it.

You have not because you ask not.

Jeremiah 29:12-13: *"Then shall ye call upon me, and ye shall go and pray unto me, and I will hearken unto you. And ye shall seek me, and find me, when ye shall search for me with all your heart."*

7. **He was open to opportunity.**

Initiative, innovation, effort over and above the eight hour day! Work hard, be creative, and be ready for anything!

Opportunity tends to come when you do your best. Sometimes when it knocks, it taps on the door very lightly, so pay attention!

A world of people want success just like you, but without a godly value system, they twist and turn (and worse) to get there. You want to get there the right way.

Be ready when opportunity knocks.

8. **He made good use of his time.**

There are many ways to serve: service clubs, church, neighborhood associations, etc. This, too, is a door the Lord wants to open. Some people don't look up enough to see it. Service to others rests you from the routine of work. It extends your influence and gives you new perspectives. Be open to what the Lord would have you do, and spend your time wisely.

Whatever your circumstances, you can live this kind of life!

2 Peter 1:4-8: *"Whereby are given unto us exceeding great and precious promises: that by these ye might be partakers of the divine nature, having escaped the corruption that is in the world through lust. And beside this, giving all diligence, add to your faith virtue; and to virtue knowledge; and to knowledge temperance; and to temperance patience; and to patience godliness; and to godliness brotherly kindness; and to brotherly kindness charity. For if these things be in you, and abound, they make you that ye shall neither be barren nor unfruitful in the knowledge of our Lord Jesus Christ."*

William and Sharon lived conservatively and saved for the future. They never made a lot, but they lived within their means. When they were able, they drew nearer to relatives, got acquainted with the area, and, in other ways, generally made good use of time. Time is precious; use it wisely!

Retirement began and life was good!

The house was paid for, and the car was, too. This is the picture he visually painted so many years ago. It would be a good picture for you, too! It's not fabulous wealth and luxury, but it's a life well lived. It's what your hand in God's hand can do. You need to mentally paint your picture now, while there is time to take the steps to make it happen.

Ephesians 3:17-19: *"That Christ may dwell in your hearts by faith; that ye, being rooted and grounded in love, may be able to comprehend with all saints what is the breadth, and length, and depth, and height; and to know the love of Christ, which passeth knowledge, that ye might be filled with all the fullness of God."*

9. With the Lord, he weathered his problems, and continued to make new friends and find new opportunities.

"Into each life some rain must fall." *

James 1:2-4 NASB: *"Consider it all joy, my brethren, when you encounter various trials, knowing that the testing of your faith produces endurance. And let endurance have its perfect result, so that you may be perfect [mature] and complete, lacking in nothing."* [Bracketed words added.]

God doesn't test you. He knows all about you. But He does allow tests to come in your life. With Him at your side when you wade through your trials, you emerge more mature, more complete, and more enabled to witness to those around you. "Joy" here is not merriment but an inner confidence that, through your trials, Jesus is with you!

1 Peter 5:2-4: *"Feed the flock of God which is among you, taking the oversight thereof, not by constraint, but willingly; not for filthy lucre, but of a ready mind; neither as being lords over God's heritage, but being examples to the flock. And when the chief Shepherd shall appear, ye shall receive a crown of glory that fadeth not away."*

An answered prayer is the greatest verification that Jesus knows you.

---

*From "The Rainy Day," a poem by Henry Wadsworth Longfellow

AFTERTHOUGHT

Philippians 4:6-9: *"... but in every thing by prayer and supplication with thanksgiving let your requests be made known unto God. And the peace of God, which passeth all understanding, shall keep your hearts and minds through Christ Jesus.*

Finally, brethren, whatsoever things are true, whatsoever things are honest, whatsoever things are just, whatsoever things are pure, whatsoever things are lovely, whatsoever things are of good report; if there be any virtue, and if there be any praise, think on these things.

Those things, which ye have both learned, and received, and heard, and seen in me, do: and the God of peace shall be with you."

ABOUT THE AUTHOR

GEORGE E. WINTERS

George Winters describes himself as a "simple" man who has led a quiet life. Those who know him describe him as a man with a true heart for helping people in ways that make a difference. His caring, godly spirit touches people in ways that not only bring peace and hope but can be truly life changing, when they have "ears to hear." Now he shares his autobiographical outline of the life of William Ray Houston to demonstrate the power of a prayer-filled life that belongs to Jesus Christ.

Mr. Winters graduated from Southern Methodist University (SMU) with a Bachelor of Arts Degree in Business Administration. He is retired and lives with his wife in North Texas.

www.ingramcontent.com/pod-product-compliance
Lightning Source LLC
Chambersburg PA
CBHW070857050426
42453CB00012B/2248